HOMESPUN MUSIC INSTRUCTION

AUDIO ACCESS INCLUDED

ARTIE TRAUM

TEACHES

101 Essential Riffs for Acoustic Guitar

PLAYBACK+
Speed • Pitch • Balance • Loop

To access audio visit:
www.halleonard.com/mylibrary
Enter Code
6232-0142-8323-6720

Audio Editor: Tom Mark

Produced by Artie Traum and Tom Mark
for Homespun Tapes at Make Believe Ballroom, Shokan, NY

ISBN 978-0-7935-8859-6

EXCLUSIVELY DISTRIBUTED BY

7777 W. BLUEMOUND RD. P.O. BOX 13819 MILWAUKEE, WI 53213

Visit Hal Leonard Online at **www.halleonard.com**

Visit Homespun Tapes at **www.homespun.com**

Audio instruction makes it easy! Find the section of the lesson you want with the press of a finger; play that segment over and over until you've mastered it; easily skip over parts you've already mastered—no clumsy rewinding or fast-forwarding to find your spot; listen with the best possible audio fidelity; follow along track-by-track with the book.

Table of Contents

This book contains music examples, and all of the instructional audio tracks are labeled with track icons (◆) for the ease of locating the corresponding tracks. The remaining tracks listed here contain detailed explanation and instruction for these songs.

❸ Blues Riffs In A

Let's start with some bluesy ideas in the key of A.

❹ First Series of Riffs / A Position

The first series of riffs are played out of an F chord position moved up to the fifth fret, giving you an A. These riffs are moveable ideas – they can be moved up or down the neck to play in other keys.

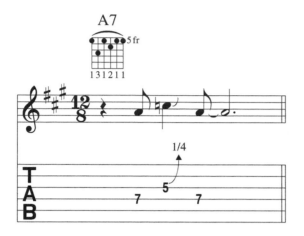

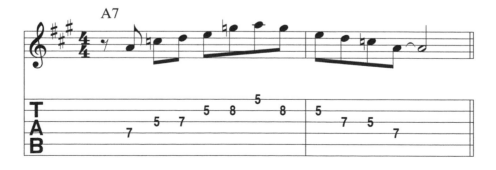

◆5 Arpeggios and Bends

What makes these riffs really shine are arpeggios and little bends. The third string on the fifth fret is a perfect little bending spot. What we're doing is bending the minor third towards the major, not quite getting there.

Another perfectly logical bending place is the second string, eighth fret:

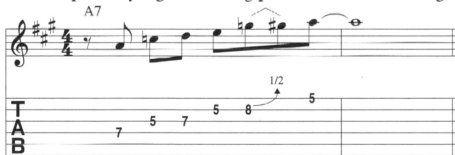

These riffs are mostly going up the scale. You can also come back down the scale:

◆6 Up The Neck

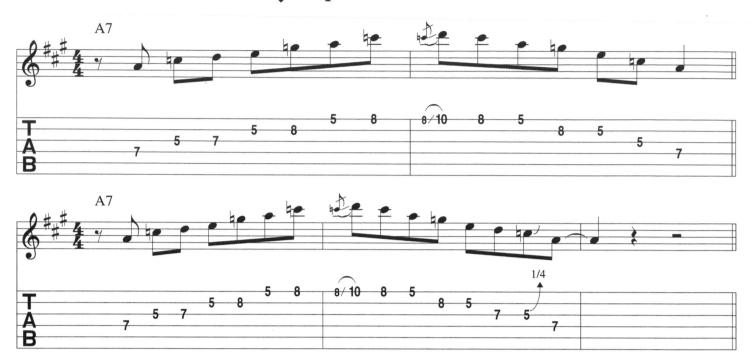

◆7 Parts Of Riffs

Let's look at parts of riffs within this note structure. On the second and first strings:

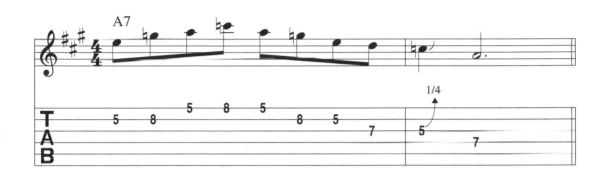

8 Series of Riffs 9, 10, 11 Fret

Now we're gonna try a series of riffs that happen around the ninth, tenth, and eleventh frets, still based in A. It's always good to know where to put a little bit of vibrato in these kinds of riffs:

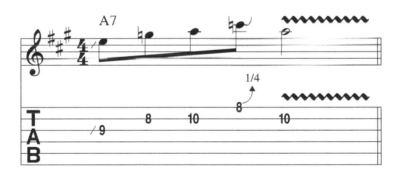

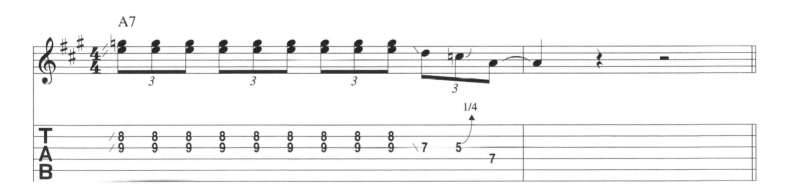

◆9 Hammering On and Pulling Off

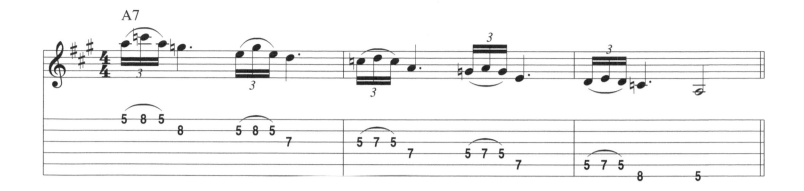

If it feels complicated or is difficult for you, start with hammering-on:

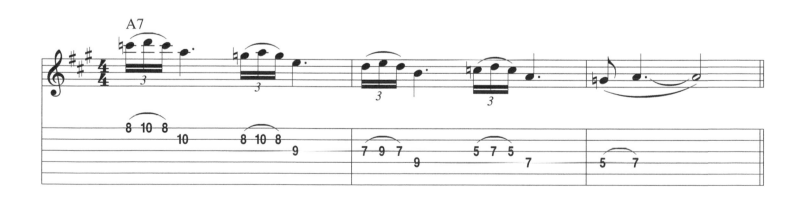

⑩ Ascending Riff Ideas

You can work your way up these kinds of notes by using your pick a little bit more:

Keep in mind that these riffs are very moveable. You could go up to B♭ by moving up one fret, and these riffs would work just as well. You should try them in all different keys so that anywhere on the fingerboard feels comfortable to you.

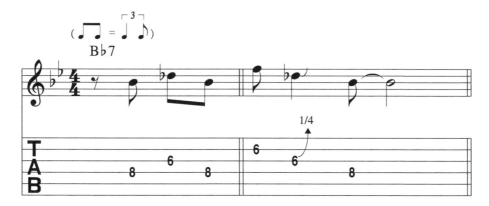

⑪ Major Scale Blues Riffs

The other part of playing blues based on this F position has to do with more of the major of the chord. I'm sure you've heard this riff before-one of my favorites:

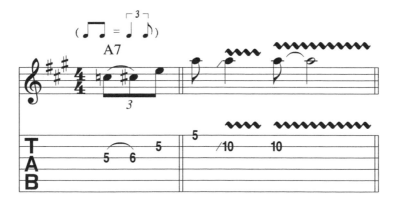

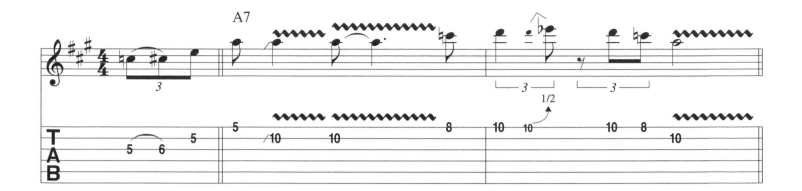

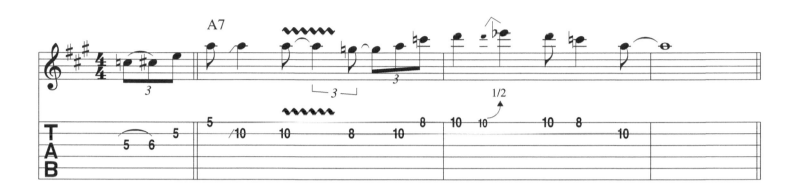

Based around the same hammer-on:

The other thing that works great around this is a slide:

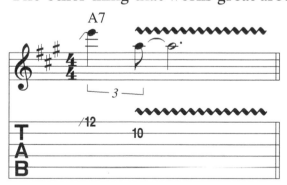

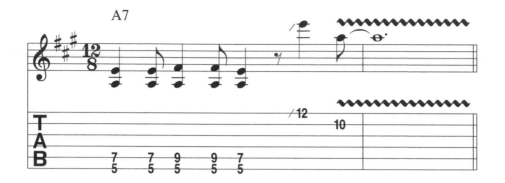

⑫ Review: Building Solos

⑬ Bends Up The Neck

Let's look at some of the bends that make these riffs come to life:

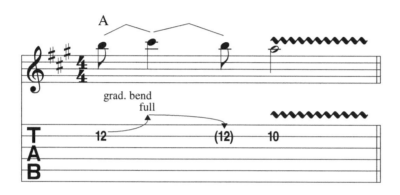

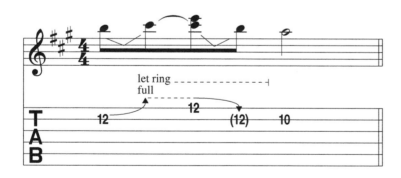

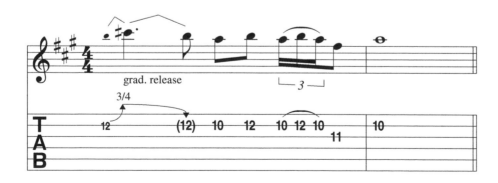

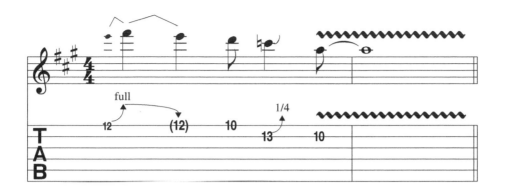

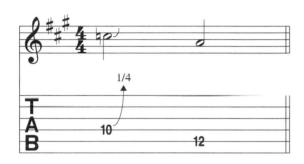

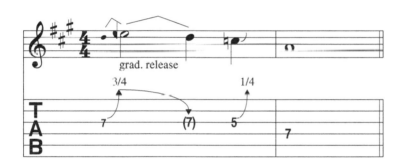

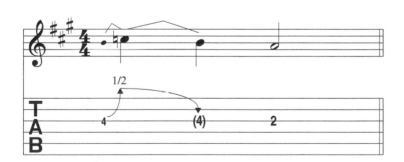

14 Bass-note Runs

Here's a really good one to practice your bends:

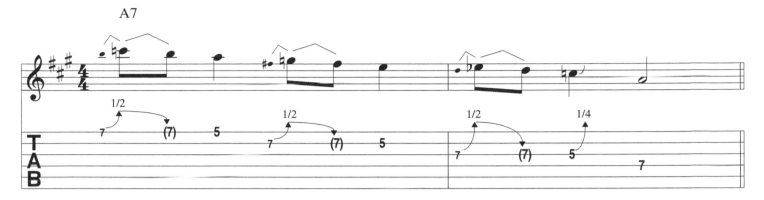

If someone was to play a blues rhythm like this,

you could start off with a riff like this:

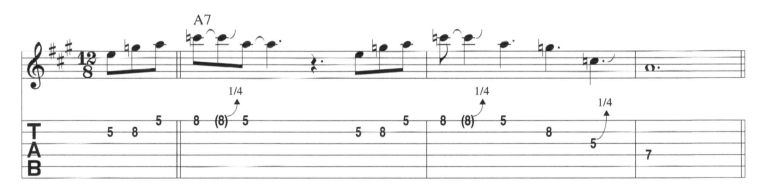

Here's an example you might want to check out of me noodling around and trying to make some of these work:

16 Blues Example #1

1st Solo

Moderate Shuffle ♩ = 76

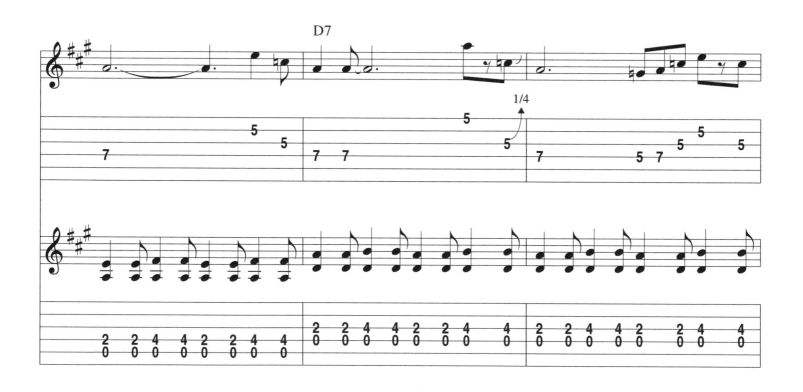

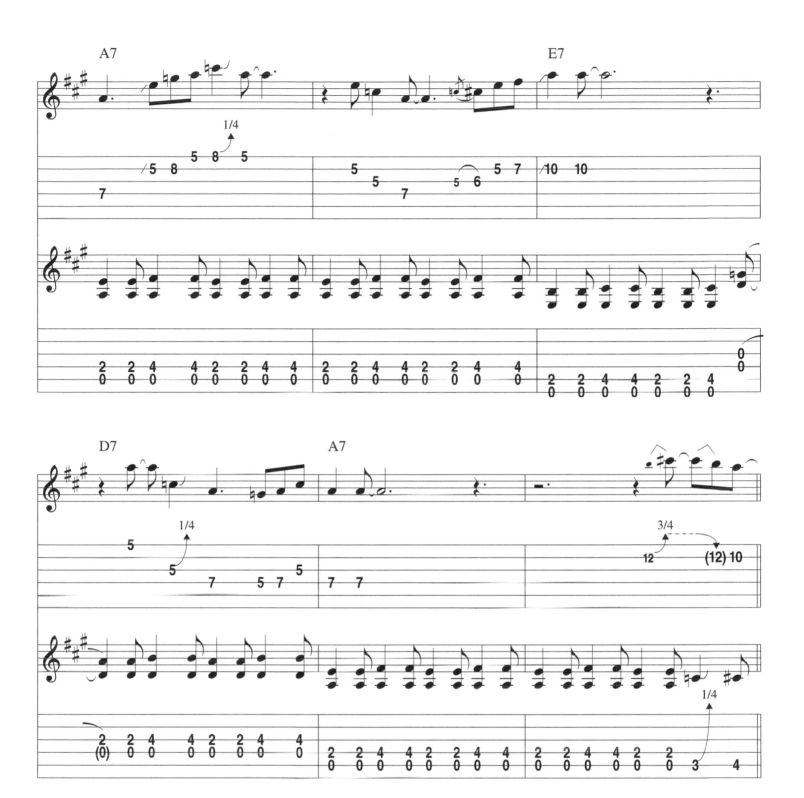

2nd Solo

Gtr. 2 cont. accompaniment simile

Gtr. 1

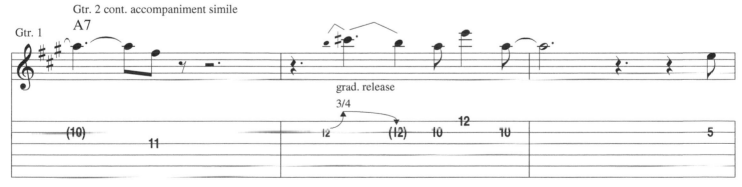

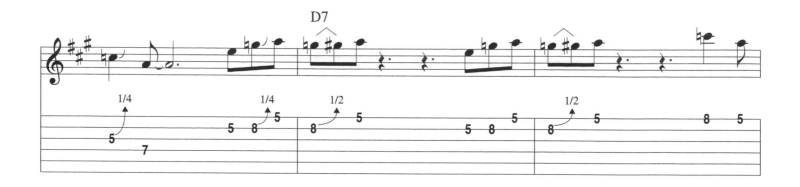

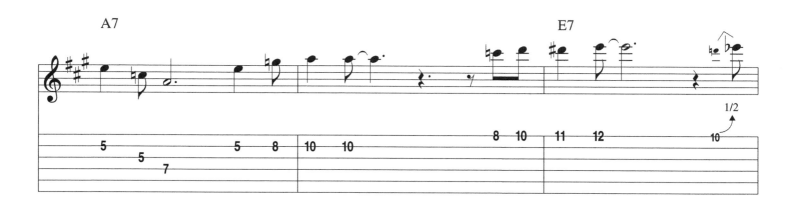

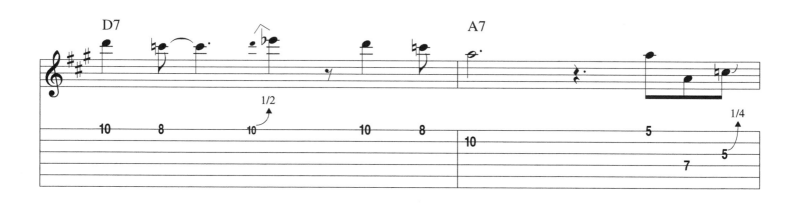

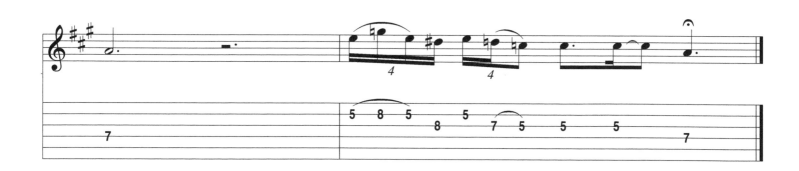

17 Blues Example #2

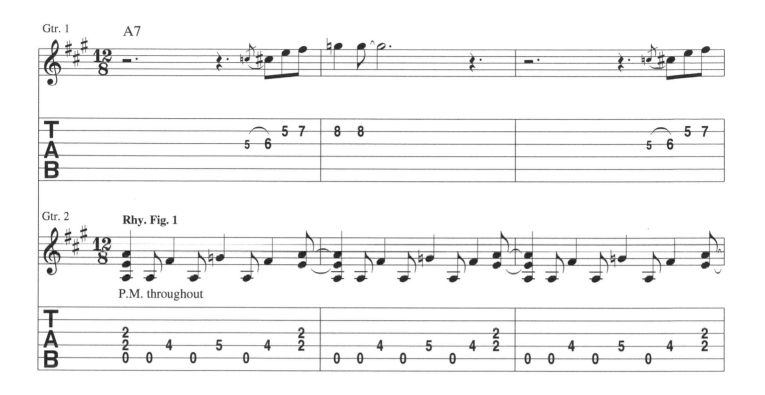

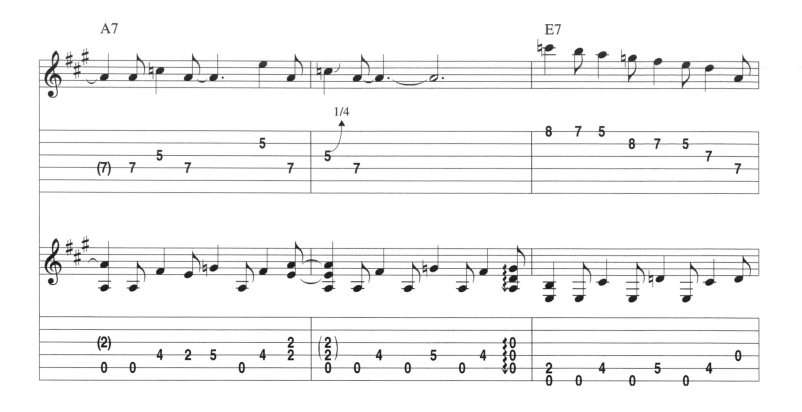

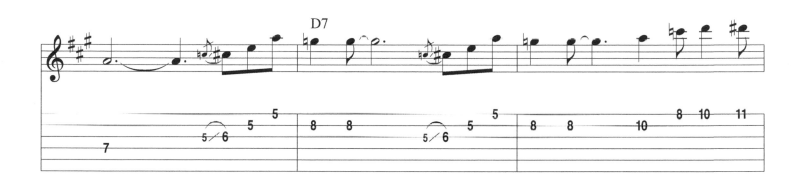

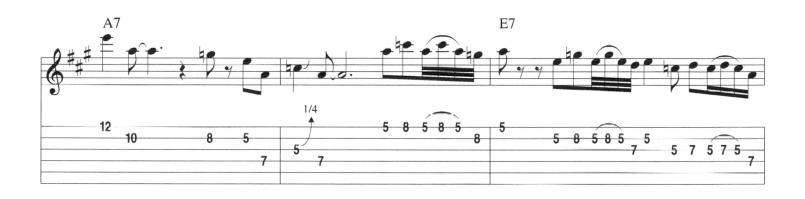

Key of E – First Position Ideas

Basically, we are in an open position, so to get these riffs doesn't require as much work.

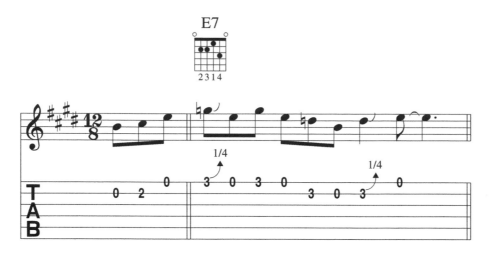

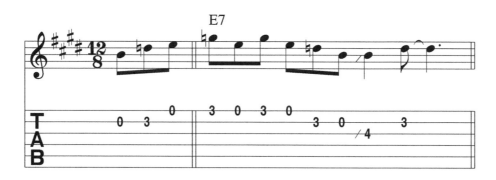

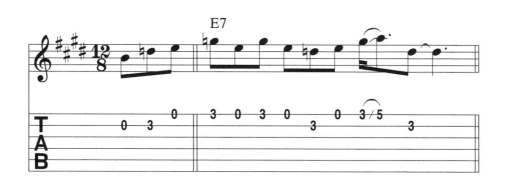

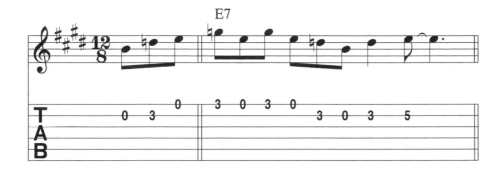

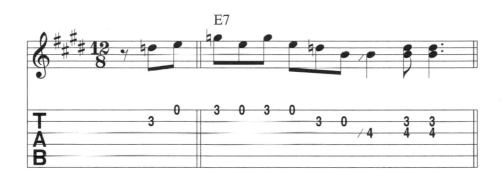

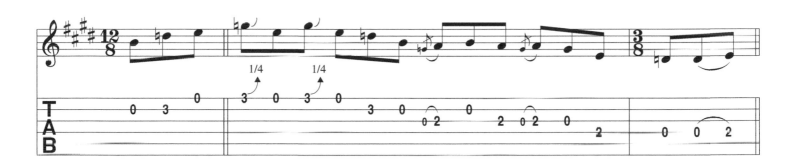

You can see that sliding and hammering-on plays a very important role, even in these open positions.

19 Bass Lines In E

You can, starting on the E position, work your way up, almost like playing a boogie-woogie line:

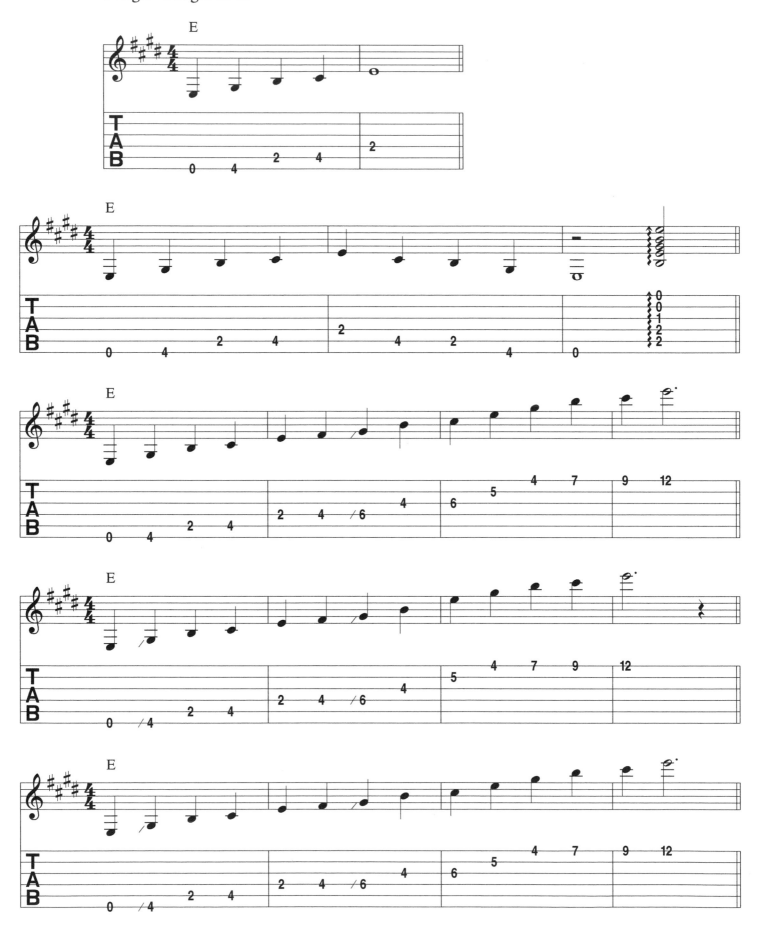

Even part of it works really beautifully:

You could even fill in some of the notes like this:

These are moveable - if you're in the key of F, for example, start with the closed note, to get the same effect:

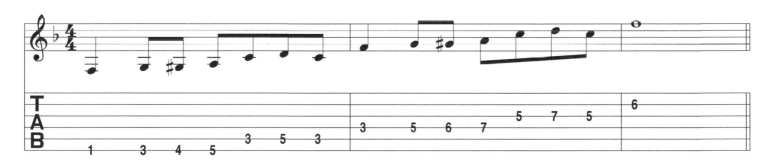

Likewise, if you're in the key of G:

◆20 Other Funky Ideas

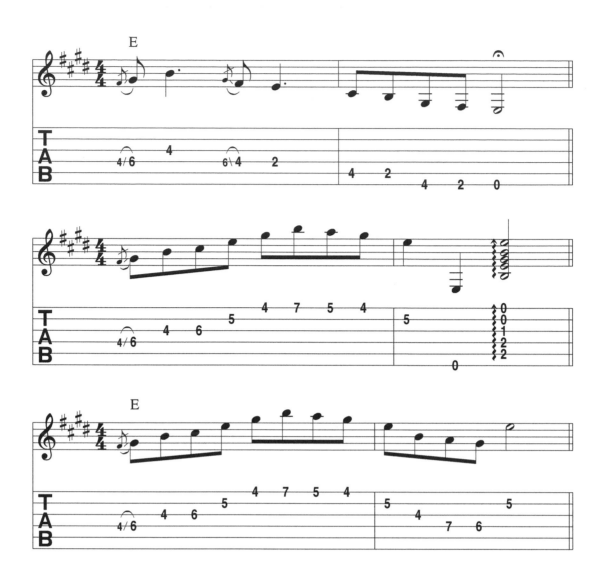

◆21 Scale From Higher E

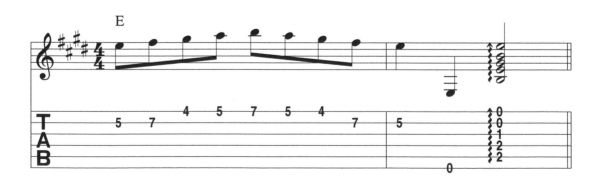

That's a very moveable little riff.

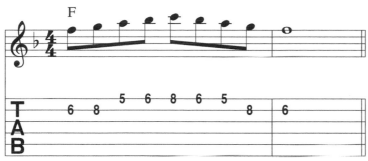

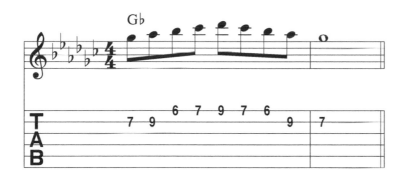

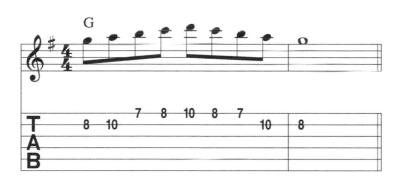

 Sliding Lines

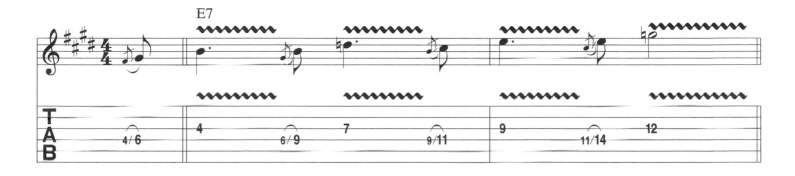

23 E Major Scale Ideas

You can also work your way back down.

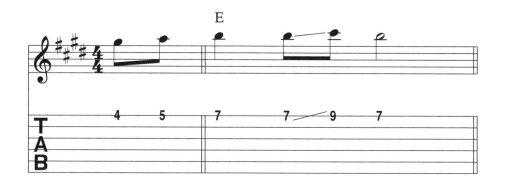

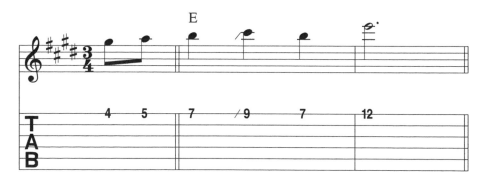

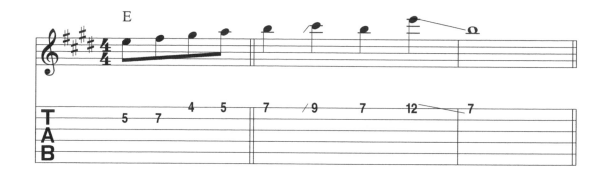

While we're here, let's try a bend.

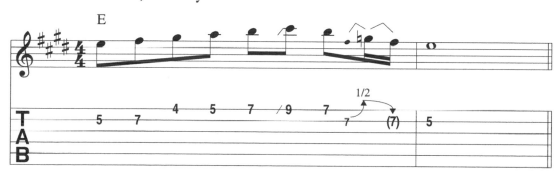

◆24 Arpeggio Ideas

Em   A7

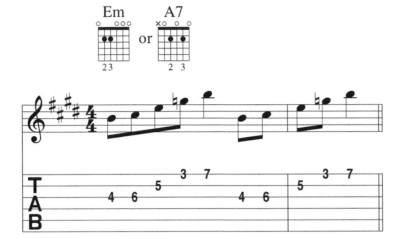

◆25 Pull-offs and Hammers

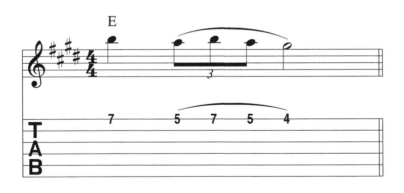

Putting these together:

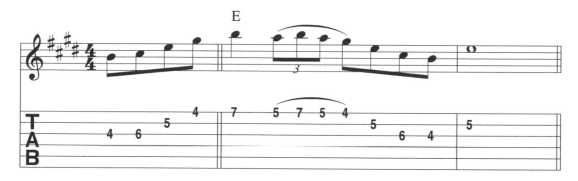

◆26 Singer-Songwriter Ideas – Example #3

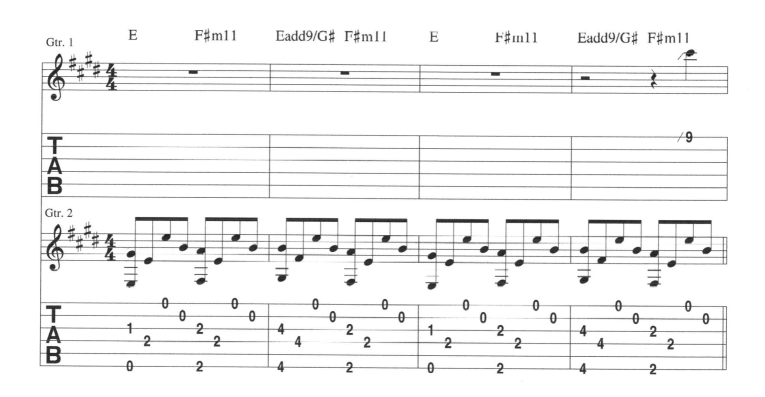

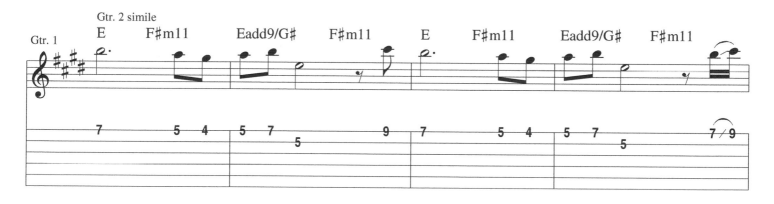

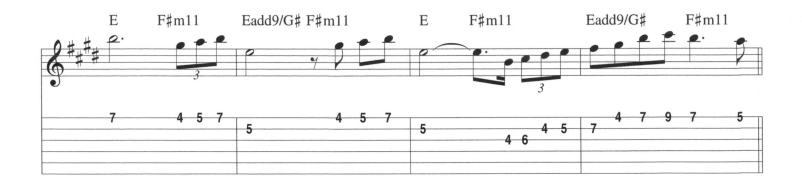

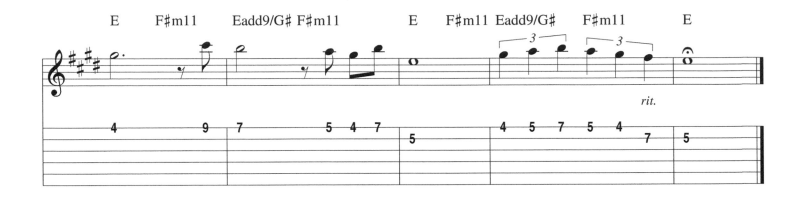

🎵27 **Example #4**

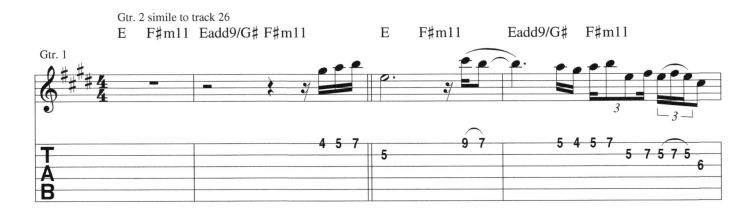

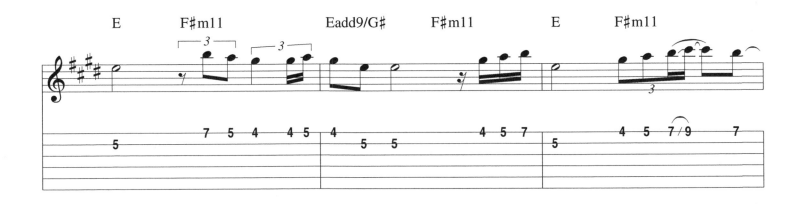

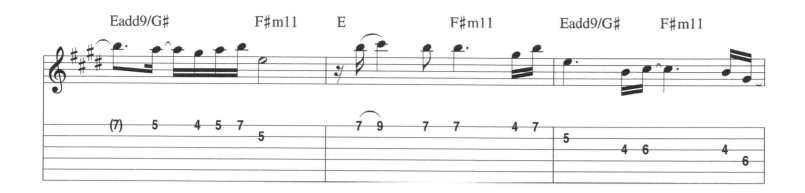

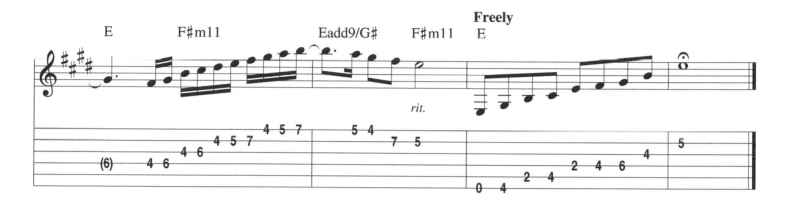

28 Minor Key Ideas

Here are a series of minor key riffs you could try:

Or, you could go up the neck:

◆29 Minor Key Bends

I love playing in minor keys because they're so rich and open. The bends work
beautifully in these keys as well:

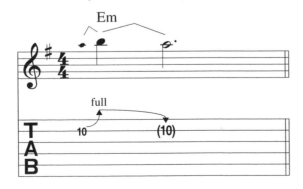

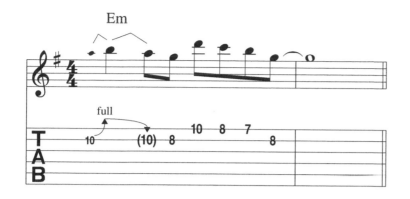

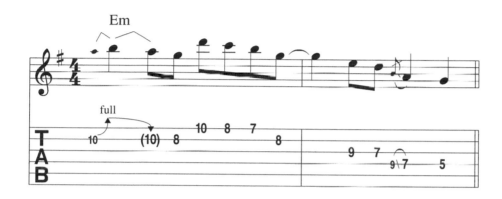

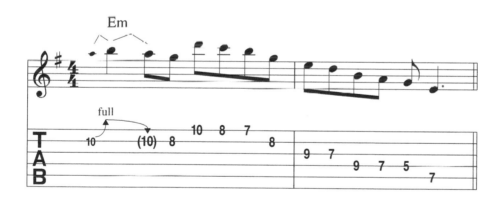

Bringing us back to the original blues riff that we did:

Voila! It works in E Minor.

So, you've got these kinds of things:

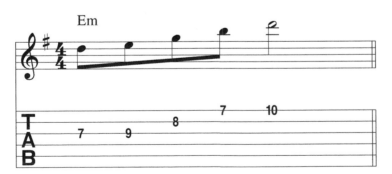

You've got the nicely articulated riffs that are nice and clean:

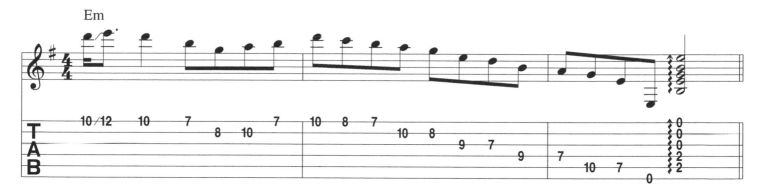

And through the miracle of modern chord work, these "D" riffs also work in a minor key. They're off of a G scale which is very much related to an E Minor.

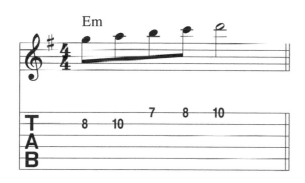

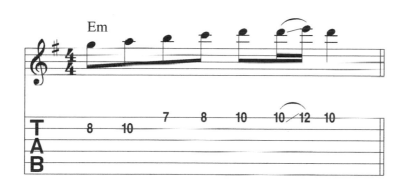

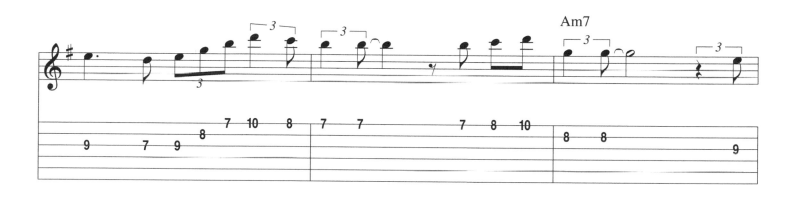

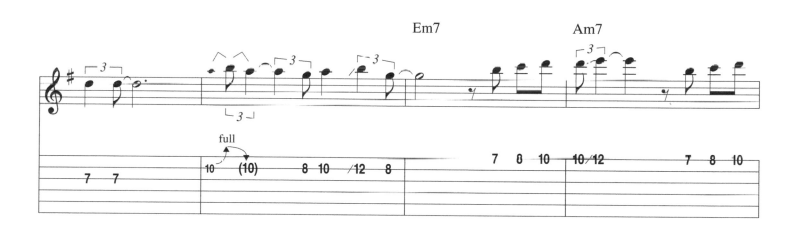

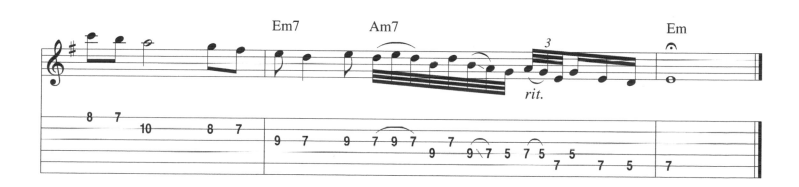

31 ▸ Introduction to Flatpicking and Bluegrass Country

This series of flatpicking ideas is chord-particular. In other words, the stuff you can do in C, you can't necessarily do in D, etc.

32 ▸ Key Of C

The open notes and chords here are very important.

33 Essential C Flatpicking Runs

◆34◆ Moving Up The Neck In C

There are also ways to come <u>up</u> the neck in the key of C:

◆35◆ Chromatic Ascending Lines and Riffs

I particularly like little riffs in C with chromatic descending lines:

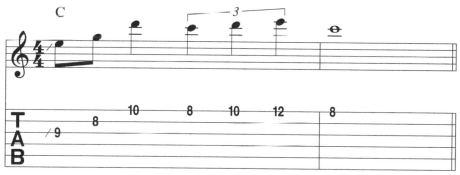 36 Ascending Off Bass Runs & Other Ideas

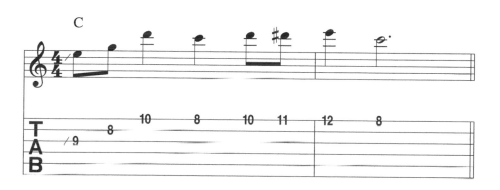

A very simple C run like this is very profound in a way because it covers so much territory:

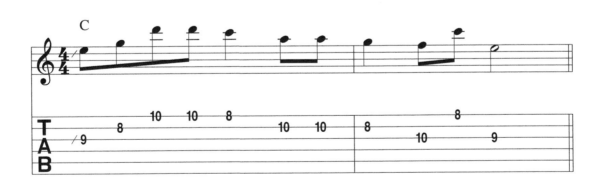

37 ◆ Further Ideas In C

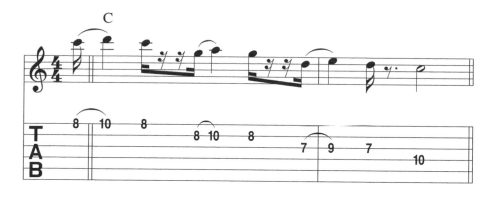

38 ◆ Flatpicking – Example #6

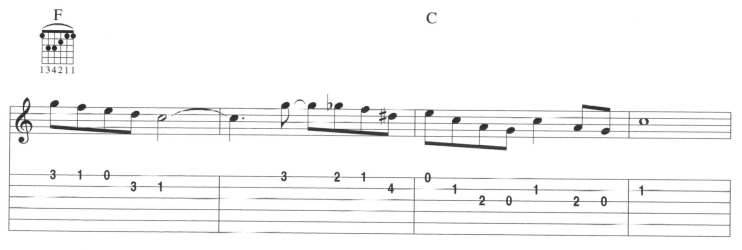

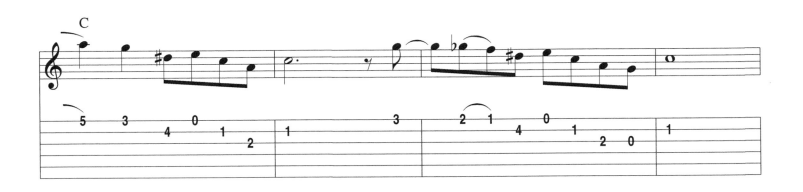

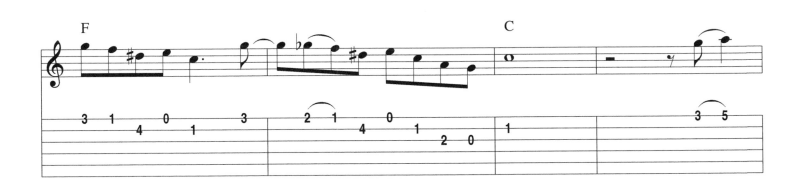

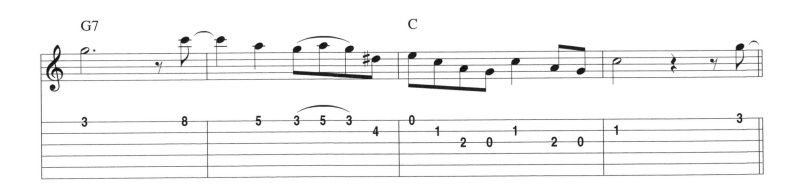

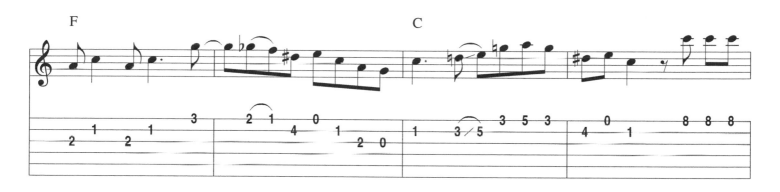

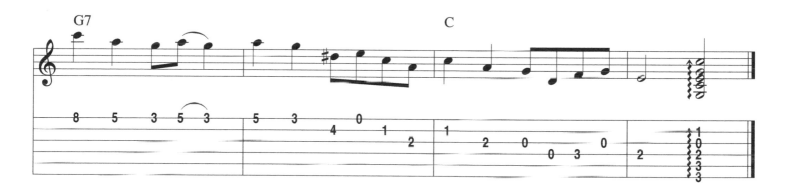

39 Key of G – Flatpicking Arpeggio

40 Riffs in G

41 Pull-offs and Hammers

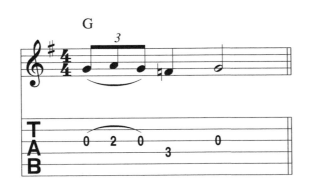

42 G Runs In 3 Positions

If you had a D position up on the 7th fret, you have all of those D chord notes that we spoke about before.

43 **Ideas In D**

You can also go up the scale.

As you study these riffs and ideas, your goal is to find where all these things lay in different keys.

44 D Arpeggio Ideas

45 Close

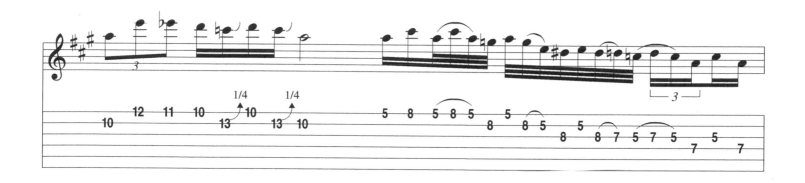

GUITAR NOTATION LEGEND

Guitar music can be notated three different ways: on a *musical staff*, in *tablature*, and in *rhythm slashes*.

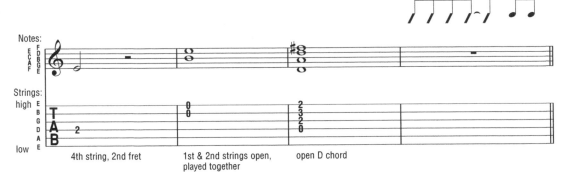

RHYTHM SLASHES are written above the staff. Strum chords in the rhythm indicated. Use the chord diagrams found at the top of the first page of the transcription for the appropriate chord voicings. Round noteheads indicate single notes.

THE MUSICAL STAFF shows pitches and rhythms and is divided by bar lines into measures. Pitches are named after the first seven letters of the alphabet.

TABLATURE graphically represents the guitar fingerboard. Each horizontal line represents a string, and each number represents a fret.

4th string, 2nd fret | 1st & 2nd strings open, played together | open D chord

---

HALF-STEP BEND: Strike the note and bend up 1/2 step.

WHOLE-STEP BEND: Strike the note and bend up one step.

GRACE NOTE BEND: Strike the note and immediately bend up as indicated.

SLIGHT (MICROTONE) BEND: Strike the note and bend up 1/4 step.

BEND AND RELEASE: Strike the note and bend up as indicated, then release back to the original note. Only the first note is struck.

PRE-BEND: Bend the note as indicated, then strike it.

VIBRATO: The string is vibrated by rapidly bending and releasing the note with the fretting hand.

WIDE VIBRATO: The pitch is varied to a greater degree by vibrating with the fretting hand.

HAMMER-ON: Strike the first (lower) note with one finger, then sound the higher note (on the same string) with another finger by fretting it without picking.

PULL-OFF: Place both fingers on the notes to be sounded. Strike the first note and without picking, pull the finger off to sound the second (lower) note.

LEGATO SLIDE: Strike the first note and then slide the same fret-hand finger up or down to the second note. The second note is not struck.

SHIFT SLIDE: Same as legato slide, except the second note is struck.

TRILL: Very rapidly alternate between the notes indicated by continuously hammering on and pulling off.

TAPPING: Hammer ("tap") the fret indicated with the pick-hand index or middle finger and pull off to the note fretted by the fret hand.

NATURAL HARMONIC: Strike the note while the fret-hand lightly touches the string directly over the fret indicated.

PINCH HARMONIC: The note is fretted normally and a harmonic is produced by adding the edge of the thumb or the tip of the index finger of the pick hand to the normal pick attack.

PICK SCRAPE: The edge of the pick is rubbed down (or up) the string, producing a scratchy sound.

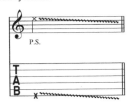

MUFFLED STRINGS: A percussive sound is produced by laying the fret hand across the string(s) without depressing, and striking them with the pick hand.

PALM MUTING: The note is partially muted by the pick hand lightly touching the string(s) just before the bridge.

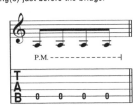

RAKE: Drag the pick across the strings indicated with a single motion.

TREMOLO PICKING: The note is picked as rapidly and continuously as possible.

VIBRATO BAR DIVE AND RETURN: The pitch of the note or chord is dropped a specified number of steps (in rhythm), then returned to the original pitch.

VIBRATO BAR SCOOP: Depress the bar just before striking the note, then quickly release the bar.

VIBRATO BAR DIP: Strike the note and then immediately drop a specified number of steps, then release back to the original pitch.

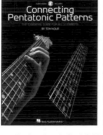

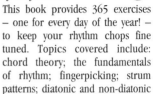

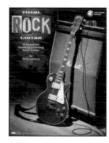